Keepsache

Books by John Hall

Between the Cities   Lincoln: Grosseteste (1968)

Days   Pensnett: Grosseteste Review Books (1972)

Meaning Insomnia   Leeds: Grosseteste (1978)

Malo-Lactic Ferment   Lewes: Ferry Press (1978)

Couch Grass   Bishops Stortford: Great Works (1978)

Repressed Intimations   Figs No. 6, Durham (1981)

Else Here: selected poems   Buckfastleigh: etruscan books (1999)

Apricot Pages (a novella)   Hastings: Reality Street (2005)

Couldn't You?   Exeter: Shearsman (2007)

Thirteen Ways of Talking about Performance Writing (a lecture)   Plymouth: PCAD (2008)

The Week's Bad Groan   Old Hunstanton: Oystercatcher (2008)

Interscriptions (with Peter Hughes)   Newton-le-Willows: Knives Forks and Spoon Press (2011)

Essays on Performance Writing, Poetics and Poetry   Bristol: Shearsman Books (2013)

   Volume 1: *On Performance Writing, with Pedagogical Sketches*

   Volume 2: *Writings towards Writing and Reading: On Poetics and Poetry, with Implicated Readings*

Keepsache

John Hall

etruscan books
2014

Keepsache: a companion selection to *else here*
Cover design by John Hall
Copyright © 1972, 1978, 1981, 2007 and 2011 by John Hall
Copyright John Hall 2014

ISBN   1 901 538-84-2
           978-1-901538-84-7

Published by etruscan books

All etruscan books publications are available from:
London Review Bookshop, 14 Bury Place, London WC1A 2JL

etruscan books
2nd Floor Studio. Oak Passage, 68 George Street
Hastings, Sussex
TN34 3EE.

www.e-truscan.co.uk

etruscan books are distributed in America by
SPD, 1341 7th Street, Berkeley CA 94710
and are available in Australia from
collected works, 1st Floor, Flinders Way Arcade,
238 Flinders Lane, Melbourne 3000

etruscan books are edited by Nicholas Johnson
Text designed and set by John Hall
Printed by Aldgate Press

Typeset by Robert Moore at *Breathe*

AUTHOR'S NOTES AND ACKNOWLEDGEMENTS

Keepsache is intended as a companion volume to *else here*, published by etruscan books in 1999. It includes further selections from three of the publications on which that selection drew – *Days*, *Malo-lactic Ferment* and *Repressed Intimations* – some previously uncollected poems, and some selections from books published since 1999. Most fully represented here is *Days*, and the selection includes a few poems that were not in the Grosseteste 1972 edition. I have made a few silent changes for consistency or where vocabulary had become uncomfortably anachronistic. A few long lines are now broken.

I thank the following editors and publishers who were responsible for the books in which these writings appeared: Tim Longville and the late John Riley for the Grosseteste Review Books publication of *Days* (1972); the late Andrew Crozier for the Ferry Press publication of *Malo-Lactic Ferment* (1978); Tony Baker for the Figs publication of *Repressed Intimations* (1981); Kris Hemensley for 'Elevenses' and an earlier publication of parts of *The Week's Bad Groan*, both included in *The Best of the Ear: The Ear in a Wheatfield 1973-76, a Portrait of a Magazine* (Melbourne: Rigmarole Books, 1985); Peter Hughes for the later publication of *The Week's Bad Groan* (2008) in his Oystercatcher series; Tony Frazer for the publication of *Couldn't You* (2007) by Shearsman Books; Philip Coleman for including the first 'rolled' version of *An alphabet for else here* in his Kore broadsheet project (2008).

Loose Packed is a collaboration with Lee Harwood, intended, in one version, to form a pack of fifty-two cards. The pack was shuffled on 20 December 2011 for the sequence presented here. My thanks to Lee Harwood for permission to include it. The source for 'Recorded Results' was *The Art Investment Guide*, Spring 1974.

I thank Nicholas Johnson for his always thoughtful work as publisher.

John Hall

CONTENTS

from **Days** (1971)

New Year (Number 1)	9
'in somebody else's dream ...' (Number 4)	10
'the dense grass in the lush season' (Number 8)	11
'I am left with what I am left with' (Number 9)	12
'the things wrong with my car ...' (Number 15)	13
'just recently my life ...' (Number 18)	14
'the accumulation from the past ...' (Number 20)	15
'today I am in love ...' (Number 24)	16
'the clean sheets ...' (Number 27)	17
'read a few pages ...' (Number 32)	18
'the sources of what we ...' (Number 36)	19
'the white pink and blue houses ...' (Number 42)	20
'the completed book-case ...' (Number 46)	21
'yesterday's mist ...' (Number 47)	22
'my letter is on the way ...' (Number 50)	23
'rain is falling ...' (Number 51)	24
'three leaves ...' (Number 57)	25
'the intimate and soiled ...' (Number 58)	26
'the second highest twig ...' (Number 59)	27
'my afternoon kip ...' (Number 63)	28
Hush Now (Number 67)	29
'I think it's absolutely wonderful ...' (Number 68)	30
'the really intense quietness ...' (Number 70)	31
'an arc of white light ...' (Number 72)	32

Three Uncollected Poems

Dream	33
Realing	34
Apple Poems	36

from **The Week's Bad Groan** (1971, 2008)	40
from **Loose Packed** (with Lee Harwood), uncollected (2008)	49
Three uncollected poems:	
Parasites	52
Elevenses	56
Recorded Results	58
from **Malo-Lactic Ferment (1978)**	
Premise	60
Firstly	61
from **Repressed Intimations** (1981)	
Coming in through the window	63
Shifters	64
from **Couldn't You?** (2007)	
Couldn't You?	66
from Gloss (Lyrical Abstractions)	68
from Here and There	
Between	71
Writing	72
Speaking and Writing	73
from Changing Lines	
'slightly smaller …'	74
'a listening you …'	76
'and all the time …'	78
An Essay on Lyric Ethics	79
from Between the Fragments	83
An alphabet for *else here*, **rolled** (2008)	87
A coda: Some Notes on Lyric and Polis (2012)	88

from DAYS (1972)

NEW YEAR

a woman walks up the Earls Court Road, past
the underground station, shouting 'fuck off. fuck
off all of you. fuck off.' a tall, middle-aged
white male (45?), standing in the mouth of the station, says to
nobody in particular but possibly to an equally tall
black male (35?), 'charming!'   'a real credit to the
english nation.' and the equally tall male says
'that's really something / else' in a deep may
be threatening voice. the girl selling inter
national times smiles to herself as though knowingly.

JANUARY
Number 1

in somebody else's dream two Friesian cows walk
very slowly up the sparsely covered hill and a wind
blows as though with the same inclining effort
bringing cold from the snow-covered moors and quiet
from the desiccated land between. it is only the absence
of the usual signs of life and a light
changing the otherwise familiar fields
that makes me think of a less evident reality
for this is merely what I see
walking with no especial purpose along
the tarred road. I have become used to some strain, an
unseasonal haste in acts as random as this
purposeless walk, and this movement of natural agents and the slow
working energy of the cows reminds me
of an old man I admire who counters a contrary wind
or a steep slope with the same slow use
of his considerable remaining strength.

MARCH
Number 4

the dense grass in the lush season
moves in unison, indolently, at the direction
of a not very commanding
south-west breeze, reminding of a tenderness
made possible by the hard fact
of even this gentle
and watered land. buttercups
'n daisies have their heads in the air
& move them about as
though the underlying shape of the soil
were no affair of theirs & this
is the freer element
they wish for. as for me I pretend
the very same thing, taking delight in this nonchalant
abundance of soil, rain & sun, in which the lavish growth
of every green & coloured thing
declares its own necessity, absolutely beyond argument.

all those anxieties of the winter
about jobs & even poems
don't matter very much
in this freer medium. the absence of grief
carries in the wind, changeably, as though
I expect it back, a melancholy refrain
telling of the brevity
of the lush times. but butter cups 'n daisies
are the common-place of the season
and I suppose don't matter much
whatever that means.

JUNE
Number 8

I am left with what I am left with
a sediment of the mixed days
and years I suppose I could call
'more fortunate', but why shouldn't I
change the metaphor a little & talk of an
'essence' or 'abstraction' from those times, if they were really
more fortunate and not just more fun. that would be
more orderly & altogether more noble, the way nobility
can be found in the most improbable places, so that even a mere
poverty of will can become a refinement of spirit, the 'man
himself', stripped of his 'delusions' I think
it goes; one of those ideas that come to us
when we're feeling comfortable & sufficiently without delusions
to be in fit shape to set out, deliberately,
in the direction of this more
noble condition. but the falling momentum of earlier activities
or lack of them isn't really like that, there is never
a precise fix on this 'I' except as the consequence
of deliberate refinement, but some commitment from an earlier
& theoretically abandoned time not only remains to be paid,
like a mortgage on a house, but is actually one of the things any of us
define ourselves by, even in the
ignoring of it. this bare-forked creature still has to eat
and likely as not will find some less strenuous means of doing so
than law evasion.

JUNE
Number 9

the things wrong with my car
are easier to talk about
than the things wrong with me, less
intimate perhaps, but more intimate
than other people's cars. the things
wrong with other people is
the best subject of all but needs always
the right audience, easy enough to gain
where we are all intimate
with each other's defects. the audience
for the conversation about the
things wrong with me
must think about it as I would like to
as offering grounds for a more intimate
and flattering interpretation. so the surroundings
must be quiet and the conversation
not overheard the which conditions
are not at all necessary
for the things wrong with my car.

JUNE
Number 15

just recently my life has become a struggle
among other things
to keep talking when I'm asked to and even
when I'm not and never to say anything
that isn't really quite true.
this seems to mislead everybody and makes the people I talk to
think I don't like anybody at all ('people'), when actually
I like almost everybody, and like everyone else
muddle along, accepting whatever help
is convenient and trying not to do anything
stupid, though most of the time this means
doing hardly anything at all.
I don't want anybody
whose life has become (or always has been)
a struggle to obtain more 'simple'
and 'necessary' things
to read this if it makes them feel
I'm being a little specialised, but then
it isn't any less a struggle
for that, is it?

JULY
Number 18

the accumulation from the past, being itself various, what can we expect
and even hope for, but that our lives
should remain various, or rather just that they will, unless
we do something singular
to end the variety, which seems
most unlikely just now. I start so many letters to friends, 'I don't
know what I will do', being careful to set this hesitation
forward to some half-specified future date and even more careful
never to say 'what to do', because that would suggest
more confusion than I like to think there is and might invite
advice, which I don't care for. besides, I *will*
be doing something and nothing is ever totally
regrettable, if only because we've done what we've done and that
lives in us and it would be foolish to regret
what we are, and the alternatives in the past
certainly aren't clear now, even if they were then
which I doubt.

JULY
Number 20

today I am in love with a girl
who isn't here. I reflect on her absence
because it remains with me, to be
reflected on. because it's a Saturday
I can choose
what to go about doing
while my memory's engaged
this way, though I always do
have something to do, like taking the letters
to the post, past the apple trees, beneath
which and on which apples lie.   on the air
something rather like apples
also lies, there is a fruitfulness
not yet plundered and outside the gate the people's
faces appear to expect the same thing
so we give it each other, readily, 'good morning',
the words lie between us and on the common
ground, at our feet, and we look down, each
as though to say, 'that might be
useful, some time'. ah I am hungry
and need my breakfast, the apple trees
are apple trees, I live with them. I love
the girl and know intimately
the path to the post-office.

AUGUST
Number 24

the clean sheets
of my newly-made bed are
desirable to me being so
tired ah but empty

of all but the promise
of sleep, in which nonetheless
who knows I may rejoin those I
love or hate or to
whom I am possibly
indifferent

AUGUST
Number 27

read a few pages
take a little walk
getting through the day
in sequence in order
to get through the night
the next day. something
not much more than
survival the intention, at
worst; at best to go
to bed with at least
a smile on my face

AUGUST
Number 32

the sources of what we, being alive, call 'life' – (love) –
do dry from time to time and at those times only that which is hardy in us
persists, along probably with the doubts and frets caused by our
'need' for that love. a poet – no, *anyone* – may be in love
with no man or woman and yet the source
may remain free to him because he 'loves' the world in all its
shape and detail. how can he say he is 'interested'
in the people around him if he is not in this way
'in love', for isn't the attention of a lover always *particular*
causing him (or her) to stand outside of him- or her-self
ecstatically in order to observe the exact movement
of the face and body of his or her
loved one, as he or she says the words that will be recalled later
in an exactitude of re-attention? it is in this sense
that we are of the world when we speak of it in an effort
to recede from the tyranny of its unbroken continuity
            and remind it and ourselves
that how it's constituted and what is happening on it haven't
been forgotten by us, and like
       true lovers we contradict it from time to time with
'but that's not what you said at all!'

                  SEPTEMBER
                  Number 36

the white pink and blue houses seize the autumnal light
to pose rather coyly, disposing the purple moors over their shoulders and
indicating before them recently harvested fields in which flocks
of seagulls wander around with a relaxed air of purposefulness,
but then are the houses really the subject-matter of this post-card
                                                                                    or is it rather

the time and the light: anything
that enters the frame moves and the shutter just clicks away
excitedly. the softly curving spar falling to the sea at Bigbury
vibrates with the same alternating current that leaves it finally
exactly where it is, and the blades of grass which all the recent rain
has encouraged to make it look as though it's spring again stand up to
be counted, apparently, or at least told one from the other. I glance
                                                                                                at my arm
and the hairs there, yes: the same applies.

SEPTEMBER
Number 42

the completed book-case stands quite happily
in my mind in the loose space allowed for it
within the phrase 'book-case', & it got there of course
with all the usual qualifications
existing circumstances require. it fits beautifully the uneven
corner of the room it is intended for & it's still
in a darker pine than the deal it'll really be made with
because of other book-cases I've seen recently & because the joins
look neater than tenoned ends of inch deal
are likely to. so it seems simple & has only
to be done – the wood bought, carefully measured, marked,
sawn and planed, the joints
chiselled, all glued & fitted
together with much double-checking, and at each stage
imagined rather less lazily so that the simple phrase
'book-case' gradually becomes inadequate, giving over to
'this book-case', as I work on it,
building in all the necessary qualifications
the revealed circumstances require.

yesterday's mist, what a terrible effect
that almost always does have on me. on a clear night
to see the whole sky, or, as now, to
look down the valley and see
sheep in one distant field and cattle in another; there is a sense
in which we all live off this distance and are confused
by mist, or the walls of a house, or a close
human inter-relation, such as family. what
is placed at a known remove is easier
to love and draw strength from, and then, in
getting closer we *want* love – like the warmth
suggested by the moist brightness thrown out
into the mist by the lights of houses – and *wanting*
love is another way of saying
'lacking love', and when we lack love
we are displaced, or often we demand it, which
can't be demanded, or feel some special claim on it
which can't be claimed.
                        it is there or not
at all and the stars and the distant sheep
teach me that it's there and I should learn to incline
towards this fact, as the line of the slate
is here inclined, towards a love more constant
than any instance of pain or delight
tells me.
            the chaste moon circles my brows
to a tune strangely we live by, while the earth
is apparently almost covered with clouds.

OCTOBER
Number 47

my letter is on the way
bearing its love casually I hope
much as the earth's surface things
take the burden of the sun this evening
with an oblique, modest splendour.
post-office vans and trains
carry my letter towards you, moving it
in the suspense somewhere between us
where the unspoken
always is. and when
you open it you will expect
what you find there I hope and will
allow yourself to be again
amazed at the expected, as we
so often are. why shouldn't
I expect an evening like this one? and yet
the gnats take it all so calmly and I am
rather foolishly amazed. and why shouldn't I
expect your love and you mine, after all
we have warned each other? your letter
is on the way, I hope, bearing its love
casually, to enter this room
with an oblique modest splendour, as it did
last time.

OCTOBER
Number 50

rain is falling out of the sky
unexpectedly. this isn't

a capital city and the cultural life
of the nineteenth century doesn't

surround me. Frank O'Hara
walked around New York and the artists

of two centuries were his familiars. I have
Vivaldi against the rain which is

wetting the hedge-sparrows. the hedge-sparrows
have themselves against the rain which is

more efficient but leaves out
Frank O'Hara and Vivaldi and everything

else including the hedge-sparrows and the efficient roof
that keeps the rain off my poems.

OCTOBER
Number 51

three leaves
point rigidly skywards
from stripped boughs
on the apple tree

to an astonished memory

laden
with pendulous fruitfulness

NOVEMBER
Number 57

the intimate and soiled
folds of my boots on the bathroom floor
have for me a certain dignity of subject matter

the left
tilts unguardedly against the right, as the design
floods with affection

NOVEMBER
Number 58

the second highest twig on the hedge
shakes on the impact of the alighting
sparrow and keeps
moving under the movement of that creature and
against the wind. I find within me an exactly
corresponding movement of the hedge and the sparrow, the same
fitful and activating wind, and the two
sets of images
move together in perfect time.

NOVEMBER
Number 59

my afternoon kip on this Christmas Eve
seems to have taken the world outside
completely by surprise. the wet clouds
have moved on, leaving in their place
bright, lighter ones, not brilliant but subduedly excitable and
the expectant moistness shines off the road, laying
itself all over the greenery so that the air
is tuneful with 'look how refreshed
everything is by your absence'. I breathe it in more
self-consciously, being rather surprised
at the accidental pleasure, and recalling the dream
I'd left it all for I breathe that in too,
which helps even more, bringing on a chirruping bird here and there
the lights in the decorated room
of the house I'm passing.

DECEMBER
Number 63

HUSH NOW

I was so tired and turned
to you on the station
a little afraid I think

you moved threateningly
in your life towards me just then
I don't know if you know that

sleep was what I wanted
and couldn't get
my thoughts had been of your arrival

it was clumsy of me to turn to you
as if saying, my love
wears me away

DECEMBER
Number 67

"I think it's absolutely wonderful
that you're in love and absolutely ghastly
that you have ulcers. What job did you have
that gave you ulcers? ... You talk
more of your ulcers than your love
which I am curious about
though I don't want to pry."

DECEMBER
Number 68

the really intense quietness of the light
snow over the locked soil
is equally without desperation

JANUARY
Number 70

an arc of white light in the western sky
lifts itself above the assembled lamps of the
large city & shines someone said
as a promise that there shall be no more
loneliness. knowing that city I don't
believe anything it says or I say
it says. over the fields
between me and it burn the more
particular lights of a few bulbs
in farm-houses I also know and whether
they be lonely or not who
burn those bulbs I
don't know that either.

FEBRUARY
Number 72

(Three uncollected poems)

Dream

in the deepest waters of night
float the faint illuminations of the stars
whose light spills
out of time
how else

do we know the dark
skin that burns in the night
or the blue coral flower
of some dark need
in your breast   in your dream

Realing

It is a room whose furnishings
have been collected for another time
and place. They have been
moved in and they will be moved out. This is my own
situation too. I sit opposite a television set no
one ever uses and listen to Sgt Pepper
because that was on top of the pile. Someone else
has drawn thick curtains to close the room
in on itself or me, which excludes most obviously
the road, the cars going from one
part of London to another, which seems
a capricious thing to do, much like listening to the Beatles
because they are there and just not hearing the song she's
leaving home. At least I assume they're
going from one place to another, though
I don't see why I should, without any real evidence
for such purity. For example today
I took a job and applied for another and I can't say
that I *want* either of them and any *need*
I might say I have for them complicates
me right out of this room, where a job
is as shifting a currency as the pound
sterling, just some arbitrary means towards a currently
authorised demand. But that's far from this room and maybe
where I should be. Nobody out there took their petrol
at gun-point – or at least if they did some
metaphor keeps them removed from the act. And so I
need a job. I'm being 'realistic'
when I say that, which means I make the same assumptions
about the terms of 'the world' as Callaghan, Wilson
and Jenkins do, and their language
is the current real, so much so that they take it
as given, ignoring the real world, royal in its
fact and possibility, which persists (exists) as that

larger term which sustains me against the deprivation
of those common assumptions.

And yet I take what's given too, even
make some effort to get it, and it is this
tells me, and the faces in Fleet Street
at lunch time also tell me, of the deprivation
that we continue to take (with thanks) that
is insistently handed at us, and who
really gains by this, so we could separate them
from the first person there? It is true that there are those
who are least victims and that it is they
who operate the mechanisms
of power, which means that the most ignorant
have the most power and it is this ignorance of the real
which is the chief tyranny. This is the barter
we allow to define our worlds and to set limits which
in any other case would be real enough
to the substance and actions of our lives.

Apple poems

(i)

I keep the company
of the articulate dead, whose remaining
purpose is to talk to us
of their living. I also keep the company of the living,
naturally, otherwise would not be interested
in the dead. I listen to each
and talk back. no one
will silence any of us, because we talk
in the company of the dead
with those who live
now or at any time. don't ask me
why this is.

(ii)

the apples
lie where they fell.
        they are
each you could say
in their most apt place, ripe
for a proper decay. no one
has touched them, though birds
have eaten and the evening sun
lights up their roundness, tactfully, so they
have never before
been quite how they are now. the grass also
rests with an unmoving carefulness
under them, causing spiky shadows
to be cast on the underside
of their shiny red cheeks. they are
still lying there.

(iii)

the child in the photograph
is my sister's daughter. she
gives some measure to my ways
by being there, since any child's
expectancies are present matter
and can resist
other sentiment. the people in the room,
except for one I love, appear
not to know this: all our acts
act also on that one, our
conversation bears in on
the child not yet born, but clearly schemed
in the womb of one of them.
I write a poem
to add to the photograph
the form of love
she casts into the room and we both
look at her for what isn't
being talked about. there is always
another love or world
beyond this one, so the poem is never
a complete
statement about anything.

(iv)

the first fruits of someone else's
(my mother's) work, the tenderest
garden peas, come to me
because I am alone
with these and all the other fruits
in the garden. I did nothing
to help grow them, I am her son, it is
a simple sentence and the love in it
leaves the account unspoken: shall I
also go beyond myself
to return elsewhere
the love
formerly passed to me? there is cruelty
in any likely answer,
and loss.

THE WEEK'S BAD GROAN (1971, 2008)

Norma Winstone with the Mike Westbrook
sextet
singing my nights have grown so lonely rather
beautifully

yes one is perhaps certainly alone
but an instrument of no mean
of no 'meaning'
something rather fine like Norma
Winstone's voice

something normal never wins
with the sextet growing
perhaps lonely under the lights
unlike my like
or light the lonely cord hanging
rather grubbily over the bed head
ing towards another working week

weak and heading back to
the working week's bed through

not snow-drops on the road-side
but snow dropped and cleared
grey in the head-lights

the bed waits
grey and clear and empty. no
there are crumbs of Dorset knobs

drop into bed, head
for the few crumbs of comfort. it is
ridiculous to return to no
more comfort than that

along a road changed since
John and I travelled on it
by our lives since

the children seeing the snow or the birds
as 'freedom'.   isn't that strange.

mouths out for beauty
                attention
                love
                            in
recognizable form

recognizable as the third form
remedials, and where's the remedy or what
is beauty, what shape or form
if I revere a man like Joan Miró and
love
or beauty only what I (in this case)
make them

is there beauty in our lives? does it drop
whitely in our dreams or

white snow drops by the changeful roadside
and if we love the mis-shapen

pale flames of an unruly sun
rise gingerly over the pillow's horizon
from an indented arc

corporately they move me, the shape
they have, to a colourful
love

hollow for a concealed eye, is there
beauty in our lives? does it enter
golden through the hideous (grubby) curtains
to bounce off familiar surfaces, which we angle
do we, in obeisance for the visit

in our dreams we rolled
steadily through the darkened memories
of recent distress, and colourfully rolled
also what we woke to, a world "new" again
in an antique daily wonder

lights driving a clear way through
high banks of grubbily impending
snow

the changeful sleep dropping brightly
in our lives, moving the opening eye
to some remedy

rise gingerly to the edge
of the week
pale ginger hair caught
in the comb, left by the mirror

the Miró painting of the beautiful
lovers left out of this with the same
regret any fine thing we have found

the admired painting not quite hanging
in my imagination against the rather
grubby lime-green wall
the beautiful lovers left in the mire
of recent distress without their
favourite painter, teaching the young
who offer some corporate resistance and what
is famous about the beautiful lovers is
a certain fragility

the week's bad groan
is again depressing. the lover
contemplates the forms of love he wishes

remembering the bare wall. daily commerce
induces some hatefulness
in us. come
house love more easily. how love?
how come mercifully before the just
hostile eyes of the children

driving us towards some dream of their
freedom, gained for them in a fairy story
against their wishes

badly groaning
meekly dispersing
the template of a love
bare of all but
memory   dallying
in the house of ill
function   some of us dream
of free petrol in the MG
soaring warmly from the
fear in our eyes
(the fire in our tyres)
our tired eyes
expensively resting

invest the house with Mozart

Miró and others

a miraculous equilibrium
to our reckless lives
which hurt our pensive eyes

let us call all the dark colours
in the miraculous painting
'fear'

and with the same rigour the light ones
'love'

that leaves us without a word
for the total relationships
of all the colours

which is the shape
all the shapes have
in the painting of the beautiful lovers

let us call that 'the painting' and in the case of Mozart
'the music'

let us call this
'the poem'

shall we secure some art for our times
by being confusingly direct and calling a painting
'a painting' and even a poem 'a poem'

and taking these objects by the handle the true
complexities of articulture follow, flung

from one pile to another in shapes

known as 'shapes', or, depending on the shape,
possibly 'poems' or 'music' etc. these shapes
have the power to move.

nobody will admit
that in handling our true lives we secure
shapes for ourselves
known as Miró, Mozart, etc.

from LOOSE PACKED

(with Lee Harwood)

all those tools in the back-room
covered in dust
from when the ceiling came down
but still
ready to hand

look along the shelf
memorial things, placed and dusted
against forgetting
against forgetfulness
what they remember
changes

"ever since she left home
a strict place
she has collected her *things* around her
she *couldn't* leave them"

inventory: "found
to have been in the possession …"

♣
under a vast sky
this restless house
that road
(these tiny objects)

    ♦
    I cry out in my sleep.
    How is that?

♣
that restless scrap
a scene
on which your memory
insists

♣
what happens
if you think of the vast sky
as an airship
this is not a careless thought

    ♦
    every obdurate thing
    marks time
    marks your time

    "articulate silence"

♦
oh these hard things
these things that are built to last
their firm outlines

and the scent-like softness
of unsolicited memory

♠
take stock now
list them
these things
that are always there

♥
"saying that she was 'loose-packed',
meaning that she was highly strung
and could fall apart easily"

♣
the airship was ready
  but never flew
heaped with vanity
  and carelessness

♥
these obstinate scraps of language
each with its own horizon

why remember this?

(Three uncollected poems)

Parasites

    i

coffee with a chaser of evaporated milk
notions gnawed by notions in light fog
quiet green and its simple nightly moves
an accurate significance in this blue island
the sources persist in every particular
evidence of trickling debris and murrain travel

poverty remains the rain that falls today
terribly beautiful and also strange
campions and the dead water crashing
entering wave rivers lovely as business
where somebody else wants your possessions
your limpid shirt is for all senses

bring the various conception
know that past love has won perverse protection
actually gulp and recite the bodily litany
your tongue tripping over the warmth it finds
in the sharp moon's submerged brilliance
the cliff in two columns ahead of us

   ii

under my chest this
 green light
     choice mist
surpassing
     desert colour

a poem grows thus
    who lay
in the harmless spaces
 silent and clear

    friends
   also live
insistent and hurried
    questioning me
brown and white and black
     and all that
  reflected

green I said
    and quiet

iii

just for now turn down the volume: the distance
glows precisely. on the horizon an easy casual fleck
slows the eye to a cheerful walk, sea coast lust and silt.
the notion of the bodies is pauseless, rocking and tilting,
wheeling small bones on the basalt ridge, the nerves
deciduous: our favourite ceremonial memory honed
to a keen steel edge. scrape the memory backwards, loveliness,
deal cleanly: the route from the distance is unusually
clear. slender as the fine beast and less meek, move
with inherited splendour, elliptic moon, down the
clean lane. pollen inhabits the surface already, curves
through the darkness, into radiant beams of moonlight; specks
caught there tremble with optical doubt, something our eyes
can't quite tell us. love the object, grip your throat
with constraint. your lust is keen and tight, enters from the
distance, amplified but precise. exchange kisses. this
is negligible, a sequence of capillary passage, with lips
bruised and tingling, particles of triumphant cupidity
standing out like fine sweat on your forehead. rampant
and wild? don't kid yourself: that tactic touches
a stress in you. your furry dry mouth knows that.

iv

the rain's raw motion clogs us
we strain to quit the white day
our sighs of boredom heavier than the skies
the cat's tense weight across our thighs

heavier than the continued low pressure presence
of one callow autobiography after another
fragments of narcissus into our drawing-room
to share the warmth of our paraffin heater

this neat shy smile through blue flame
the red wine shines distortedly
our possessions are reflected there
a radiance bitterer than our nettle beer

we listen to Shostakovich on the radio
sipping elderflower wine from tiny purple glasses
the music clears the air
the wine is sweet but delicious like his distress

                                                  autumn 74

Elevenses

the day after bombs exploded in Birmingham
    we can't claim the future our right to the present
my poem cannot expiate violence
    the persuasion of ownership and wealth
stirring sugar in hot tea (past perfect)
    (post-nuclear explosion recorded on cellulose film)
the present tense is a mist in the mornings
    central Birmingham yesterday, as the gloom piles in
seen as a shortage of everything except violence
    of reflecting dust which with less discrimination
I can manage of a sentence in that

I write a poem. the hate is beyond me
    the tense is disputed by the logic
miserable with it. lack of power to dictate the new rules
    it would replace. peace is something
driving to the corner shop on a distant vaporised pain
    of a dead language east of Suez
over the river burned off by the daily need
    the present tense flips darkly to the passive voice
everything that we've already got that is
    hides the sun. a science
present tense starting out somewhere in the debris

in time, so far we actually protest innocence
    of fragmenting violence, we limp along (past continuous)
of power, gentleness as prophetic politics
    'ordinary decent people' (past tense) won't get
our children's children will feel innocent
    that what we said to each other we said
which drives us into the past. we feed off the dead
    so that we're 'ready for everything' which means
in 'standards' as the shadow of others' wealth
    fictional mist in the Dart valley reflects upwards
at the edge of an oppressed notion in Birmingham

believing that we are gentle people and do no harm
    collecting shrapnel we mistake for direct speech
needs an eloquence equal if not greater
    wouldn't know what to do with
about as wealth achieves the abstract cloud formation
    under a street-lamp our elders keep alight
and our language is as safe as a pub in
    quietly expecting the worst to happen
falls over Europe somewhere below the high layer
    just. before dispersing the only suggestion
that you can still damage the past now

                                              November 1974

Recorded Results

Despite the energy crisis which has rocked the western
        democracies, there has been no let up
                in the demand
    for works of art. If anything there has
been an added urgency for the need to change

        money into an investment.

In recent times there has been a tendency
      to talk about auction records, picture
              prices and art
    values as if the market were an entity
in itself and isolated from the world around us.

        It is not so. It is

very much bound up with our social and economic
well-being. Indeed the results recorded
              throughout the
world during 1973 have once again emphasised
the exceptional position of paintings and *objets d'art*

        as a safeguard against

rises in the costs of living and monetary
      uncertainty. The paradox lies in the fact
              that to succeed
    in the long term, one must not only
have a solid knowledge of prices but also

        a great love of

art: history has shown that the most
        fortunate speculators were first
                                of all great
        collectors and that their good
fortune was incidental to this passion

        for art.

from MALO-LACTIC FERMENT (1978)

Premise

the listener hears a language he doesn't 'understand'
and understands as he listens that this is *a* music
of his dreams   it is one of the ways he now realises
his dreams speak

his 'dreams' are quite banal nightly occurrences
but no longer so
he doesn't understand his dreams and yet he loves them
he truly loves John Coltrane who speaks his dreams

it is important to understand that the interpretations of Sigmund Freud
have little to do with this

William Blake and Gustav Mahler
their voices also from the past contract his tenses
his body is in great readiness for the present   there is
precariousness of unexpected effort all around him

his ears are almost numinous
he cannot fly
his own banal dreams are you might say a
spirit level
one behind each ear near the hinge of his jaw
he runs them nervously over the contours of 'survival'

Firstly

the numbers are not sequential
are names with the suggestion of rhythm
which is to say dynamic order   (harder!)

as coming down on the hard beat   ONE:
the point is   TWO   are any number you care to mention:
discourse is a journey   THREE
for which we suppose a destination   (A BEAT?)
and the destination is the field-mouse   FOUR
when the cat does catch it
and the leaves and grass hanging from the cat's mouth
are circumstantial evidence in case we miss the point

and of the two images in the mind   ONE/TWO
which is the *point?*

the cat crept in when the metaphor
was left open   she is a real cat
called Mingus

these images are not at all confused in time though I don't know in which
order they occurred

(ride the high cymbal, Elvin)   any number
you like
but bring it back say with the suggestion of FOUR
which the feet can use
(the field-mouse wrapped in grass and leaves)
keep the mind dancing though in polyrhythmic discourse
divide not your thoughts in four

: any drummer from Kenny Clarke in the tradition suggested
by that name and this poem
play through your mind a sequence of such drumming
behind a voice instrument: this will take time
where you place it in relation to:
        'the discourse'
       the cat
       the field-mouse
       the clump of grass and leaves
   and a poem that contains all these

is suggested only by the sequential drumming of syllables
which ends more suddenly than the rain

from REPRESSED INTIMATIONS (1981)

Coming in through the Window

He went away for a long time in the hope that when he came back everything would have changed. No! not that every *thing* would have changed but that *he* would, that 'we' would. Of course. Of course. One morning, even, hesitating at the bedroom curtains wondering which of his worlds would enter when he pulled them. Hey look! there's a ... it is a fox, a fugitive element in the scene he has fixed on, head and tail only above the barley and *of course* he looks over at the rabbits in their cropped patch of field. Watch out! The colour barley is! And a vixen's head and tail! She'll have a rabbit or two if she wants one. He's just looking, of course, and going downstairs to change windows he holds in his head the chicken run, the fox, the relative taste – as he supposes – to fox of rabbit and hen. It is a habit to make of decision and anxiety an aesthetic issue. There might be something but there isn't. There isn't anything but there *could* be. Of course there isn't anything. Did he expect anything to have changed? Their friendships have lapsed in several silences but believe me theirs have been part of all of them. Why should they suddenly wish to write? He drew the huge curtains downstairs. Didn't the vixen look up at the loss of a white wall, at an opening into a recessed space? Stare? And then move off? News, as behind any screen you look at or through. He turned away from the event, the ripple of barley.

Shifters

who is the we
you
keep talking
about or as
is
the we who
talks the we you
claim
to be is
it the same
as I in plural
conviction am
I the you
addressed your
address beckons
yous and
needs me
can I
refuse I
is a way of being
absent
glyphic disguise deep
wardrobe of
authenticity like
pointing
to my chest speaking
personally I
could be
lying for
example
writing
is solitary
passing speech
through fingers in
to deferred space so

any writer is a
self defined
by latent contact
when
the I becomes we
there is implied
a community
of interest
I am addressed
as you
by a we whose
skill
is words
what he or she (they)
make (manufacture)
is language (they)
advert our attention
to alien
goods our
is possessive

the you I
address
is the one
who is listening
speech makes you
a latent presence
you
are implied by
my
self and all
the others
more
than that I
don't know
you

from COULDN'T YOU? (2007)

Couldn't you?

In those golden days the talk was miniature and barred: under-stated, precise, golden and, when appropriate, just not stated at all. No voice was raised, even in silence. It was then I learnt how various omission and restraint can be and learnt to admire and envy – indeed try to emulate – articulate silence.

I could never get past the part in the story where they all left. A loss is not a loss unless it keeps happening. Perhaps there is a time when you are just about to lose the loss and you remember, poignantly. Like waking with a start just before you were asleep. The point is not when they left but repeating to yourself how it will be when they have gone. It will be all right won't it? No it won't. It is because you can't forget that it will happen again. Once is enough but there is no such thing as once. Once upon a time happens all the time and is impossible. It can't happen. The time which never was has gone and what repeats is not the time but the impossibility of its return except as a sense of its impossibility. What repeats is this avoidance of this story of loss. It has to repeat impossibly because it has no history. It is avoided so often it is fully there. Hung by the force of avoidance. And what hangs swings. At every moment returns to itself in order to leave for itself. It is not as though I could tell it once and for all. Though I could try. Couldn't you.

Despite a severance, solemnly to declare veracity and perseverance. Hit verity and back down from teeth on lips to front palate. Suppress palatal terror. Palatial errors, with flowers and vowels free-ranging over the lawns. Parkland commandeered for the purposes of modern myth. Majestic common land. Tell me I'm not wrong. Travel between vowels and prefixes through the oscillations of cut-and-run, of truth on the move. She smiles shyly because that's the way she was stolen. An old trick. If you can't say it sing it. The young charmer. More than half in love with you singing. Repetition of white teeth chanting against red lips. Truth grows delirious. Heaven knows what the doctor got up to meanwhile. Trembling in the face: teeth and lips. Paid to cure. Caring about that. Lying because you care about cure. Of course truth bleeds loss and blossom on the lips. That's the smile that severs. Spit the tooth out to say it. Why not? Truly, you'll smile later through the gap.

∞

There is repetition and there is avoidance. There is avoidance of repetition. The avoidance of repetition is repeated. You don't notice perhaps because your attention voids itself, veering on to the surface of particulars. On to *the* line of events. This is how you love and avoid love. There is no object larger than the imagined world. Its worn corners. Its weary shoulders. Love repeats on itself. This abstraction is a loop out of the real that holes out local meaning by senseless repetition. Say it often enough and it empties. If you empty it carefully enough what is left is a fine abstraction, a void or vacuum pulling back the gravity of particulars. As though a nothing could exert such force. I repeat myself. Of course I don't. It is suspended by a force of insistence. On being nothing.

∞

there is repetition
I could never get past
there is repetition and there is
I could never get past the part
there is avoidance of repetition
I could never get past the part in the story
the void dance of repetition is repeated
the lost last part in the story where they all
I could never get past

from **Gloss (Lyrical Abstractions)**

remorse

you did it
          it
bites back

                        shame

                    you wish
                    you had
                    n't you
                    did it
                    shows no
                    way to
                    look a
                    way wound
                    is
                            ever
                    ywhere

    envy

        your lack
        in sight o
        o ther's full
        ness

                          diffidence

                      hang back
                      (hinge)
                      but hanker

irony

wound mouth
wound not
un
wound from
site
of speech

affection

        facts s
        often
        looks di
                late
                      lassi
        tude of good
        ness pull
        s love near
                haze
                      y and you
          phoric

possession

no good
ness
when love close
s
in
on the lo
        ok to
break
    and enter

bitterness

        in mouth where sweet
        ness
        end
            s the debt
                        me
        lancholy
                wo
                      n't pay

yearning

in the eye a
fleck no
less
than a store
y of
  of loss leave
the fullness you
never had the
facts soft
end their sur
faces perm
e able

tenderness

        breath missed
        ing mem
        ory: you will
        re
        member
        this

from Here And There

BETWEEN

where is a car enclosed space german solid moving and not moving doubling at least the heres the one I'm in and the ones I pass that relativity of passage between here and there troubled with a where except when you know it so well and then the heres on the radio moving around all over the place an anecdotal world intruded heres and others that determine the cost of this journey I make its safety too do I feel safe yes and no these are not corners you can see around and some of those supposed to guard my safety scare me on this journey to and from work to home home to work as though work was still a place as it is with car parks to prove it and in both directions a cranial enclosure where I think I think ahead or behind like the old song not an adventure pitched at a future but the circuit of a repeated present pulling a future back each twist into its turns sing it again everyday knowing the rhythms stops lifts drops and turns again these rehearsals of prepositional movements and internalised imperatives leave home turn left up the hill then right watch the crossroads with the blind bend to the right and the flood too when its been raining before you see the tower of the burnt church this must be an old road to the moors from the moors to the town miss the town now these are called by-passes not *to* not even *through by* go down and right and left roundabouts painted on the road do the trick right and left and then a long run crossing the Dart twice because its turns are different from the roads and left at the church thirty miles an hour on average little to do with tempo more timing not swaying to its going arriving is only temporary

WRITING

heart felt a scattering and a gathering heart ease the heartlands the veldt these artisan processes whose conflicts hurt first take these graphs and make of them a sentence why it is a very long way from sentence to letter parse it down no further it is graphic and heart felt and you don't know if this is something you saw or heard what you hear are parsed pauses breaking hearts in many places again and again and as you tease this out you wonder if it is the same place of damage here place is a sound and a vague shape in your body about which you can sometimes say here it is just here and that it hurts or you hurt as soon as you say you it is all of you a whole place for others say that you hear nothing in these circumstances except a sob one sob say and it all goes quiet it may or may not be you sobbing it may be a he or a she who sobs and it may be a one who sobs and so an it and that it is not quite you though your heart is not as quiet as the room is when you think this because everyone in the room replays that one sob in anticipation stopping their breath but not their hearts a letter cannot escape the heart by way of the mouth except in translation a phoneme can it is as though a letter a single letter had escaped because that is what a sob is a single sob it is an escape from the body of one person that might enter the body of others vague and translated just below or above speech more of an escape than a sigh is though perhaps a little further from speech do you see how letters do not stay silent despite your best efforts

SPEAKING AND WRITING

who speaks who doesn't who knows here that speech isn't wanted even by herself himself see how the genders switch in the air of these imagined speakers who need another story when we have always had too many which is the same as not enough and all they do is say that this is how it is or this is how I say it is or this is how it could be the moods switching around even more than the gender proscription knowing when you should keep your mouth shut your writing fingers still although at this point it wouldn't occur to some to speak and it wouldn't occur to others not to do you practice not speaking what you cannot let out hold it there is that the same as hold it in what is it to speak aloud to nobody that body that is not you at least yet who is listening in when you write when will they hear you this is not a letter except one to nobody or everyone or that letter to a someone withheld or with the proper names all switched I am writing there is nothing ahead I am circling there is something below or within these are sentences heartbeat heartfelt words not sentences fuel and shape like john wayne in the searchers cold hot heart look what avoidance has done stiffening hardening returning to the practised distances of childhood fearing your touch exactly because I want it so much and in this sentence I don't even know who you are a touch in general somewhere no longer the touch of a named someone and this is the age-old story of age the troubled memories of bodies aged thirty in their dreams

from CHANGING LINES

Slightly smaller ...

Slightly smaller
All have red crowns
Whitish belly
Isolated black streaks
Seldom drum
Both parents share in care of brood
Resident

These centuries of the decline of ancient philosophy
Almost forgotten
The task of gathering and ordering the entire corpus
Quite natural for them
Logic, physics and ethics as their guiding thread
Hand down material not put in question

There can be no plagiarism in philosophy
A permanent type of the speculative temper
Nature as a mirror or reflex of the intelligence of man
The impress of reason
Living energy of an intelligence
Experience has gradually saddened the earth's colours for us

Could you ever say I don't want to hurt you without hurting
Pain-killing a typical metaphor
Morpheus was the Roman's god of sleep
Of quick-sand dreams
This love vague and necessary
These things that I do to show that I am here
Mourning the loss of bed-warmed skin
A device for carrying distance over sound
A ritual act against night fear of incompetence
Pray for the competence of prayer
Speaking about to begin, about to end, where blessing comes

Margins without pages
Your words give off the others you know nothing about
A listening you can assign to the dead if you wish
Your solitude is strangely companionable
You have crossed through loneliness to the other side
You have to go back, with ink in your mouth
You miss the nameable dead horribly
There is no one to tell
Your tongue moves in solitude
This could be called talking to yourself

You cross over again
You rejoin the dead if they will allow
Only as you speak to yourself
You speak for them
You speak because of them, out of loss too
Grieving the previous dead
And all the time you are blind, your rainbow eyes

You should sleep you would like to sleep
You find that you have behaved badly in another's dream
Something you do that you will not say that you do
A lover – actual or desired – hovering over your exchanges
Fails to protect hurtful data

A listening you …

A listening you can assign to the dead if you wish
        draws your words
                a lover – actual or desired – hovers over each exchange

This machine carries distance over sound
        ritual act against night
                and all the time you are blind, your rainbow eyes

You keep saying I don't want to hurt you
        even this thought hurts
                experience has gradually saddened the earth's colours

Hand down material is not put in question
        I don't know that I don't know who I am
                I should sleep I would like to sleep though not

Helplessly a wrong-doer in another's dream
        writing its black line
                those quick-sand dreams impossible

Always on a margin
        mourning the loss of bed warmth
                nature as a mirror of intelligence

As you speak to yourself
        using pain-killers in typical metaphoric fashion
                praying for the competence of prayer

As they move in solitude
        blessing comes quite naturally for them
                something you do that you will not say that you do

Your tongue is a solitary mover
        alone in its cave, protecting and rejecting data
                the impress of reason

There can be no plagiarism in solitude
        or else it is a knowledge copied endlessly
                this task of gathering and ordering

The known solitude of your body
        is gathered from others in acts that mirror love
                how should it know or love

There is no one to tell
        these centuries of the decline of ancient thought
                these things that I do to show that I am here

Talking to myself no mirror mists over
        these are two uneasy lovers
                not reducible for a moment

To ear and tongue
        the others keep returning in vague and necessary love
                you cross over again

You don't know who you are
        though as they enter and you love them
                really you don't know that you need to know this

You have crossed through loneliness on both sides
        where you find the others who love
                and where you say the dead are

You miss the nameable dead horribly
        each time you have to go back, with ink in your mouth
                you speak because of them, grieving even their previous dead

Your solitude is strangely companionable.

and all the time ...

and all the time you are
be
   coming blin
           dly impossibl
                      e,   a machine
forgoin
      g distance, lover
how your
jailor's eyes
keep tabs on speculative
listening
mum's the word
no
other
place for the
quietness of you dead who
rest in
silent
threat
under co
       ver of
whitening bone.   e
              xperience pales before
your pri
      zed silence

An essay on lyric ethics

a circuit of economics belief territorialism
a competition for the right to resources
a desk of my own
a lyric elegy for a damaged world
a noble violence
a political life-cycle of fuel
a roll call of names
a space of arbitration and withholding
a violent anti-violence of writing
a word with dance in it like chorus
an ineradicable violence

and to resist damage
anyone who isn't for us is against us
apostrophe is dramatic not lyric
as ontological destiny
as part of their job

behind me beside me above me
bracketing out particularity
but these should not be confused

can lead to systematic mass murder
constelled by coincidence into systemic evil
costing lost sexual violence

dispersiveness

epic song
everyone needs to know *who* deserves
expensive solitude
extend beyond any lyric instance

for players of musical instruments
from the ethics of lyricism

geared teleology
genealogy of comfort

having nothing to stand under
helped death workers see themselves as noble
however ceremonially restrained

I keep the company of the articulate dead
implicit violence of any belief
implies a world of the possible

in a denial
in certain circumstances
in most circumstances
in my solitude in my negotiations
in notorious examples
in the conditions of a poem

instances of individual pathology

is a condition
is certain and figures
is dangerous
is it enough that
is love or war
is lyric always melancholy does it need
is not caught up
is this sentence one of 'ours'

its surface inscribed

love takes the named as its object
lyric mobility

modal possibilities
named as a 'war on terror'
not just a competition for resources

of corporate extermination
of course there are 'bad apples' at home
of the dramatic
of the nameable
of the purity of sameness
of the right to inflict damage
of what it could be to be human
only one of which
or perhaps where drama hands over to lyric
or this *terminal* with its abstract *address*
overseen by images of male ancestry

part pensioner part employee
points at the name-holder's chest
power outpowers power

quiet like a no-reply

repeating its silence

say that each poem
sitting at a desk indirectly bequeathed
spreading freedom
stories accounts poems and arguments

take a simple lesson
take the names away and I speak foolishly
tempting into place a theology of devolved absolution
temptingly nameable

that a poem's linguistic order
that certain poems
that freedom is a right
that gives me title
that right is a freedom

the American people
the articulate absent

the mechanics and performances of power
the motor car for example
the nameable is destroyable
the right to damage in the name of this right

theologians used to know this
these conditions of lyric personae
these epic conditions of lyric solitude
this new expensive pen
this world in which *evil* is abroad
those who murdered
though as ever names double as decoys
though I have no doubt
through its exclusion of certain
throughout the world

to adopt the posture that humans do when they sing
to catch an erotics of will a violence of drive or purpose
to ignore and deny damage

transcendent subjectivity

uncertainty of circumstances
up against

violence that conceals itself

waived the death sentence
we want each other('s)
what contract of belonging
where music and poetry are concerned
where resources are always subject to contest
wishing for a better world
within a territorialism of style
within the complexity of financial regulation
within the law

yes ok co.uk

from **Between the Fragments**

To have these records! He jabbers of all this in English, stepping forward before I could send him to America, and cared nothing, saying there was this and this! Suppression is required. It was not always as it is. There is no return from this post of 'as' language – as much as America is in command at these my hands, and in the mail; but no 'us', and of the first things I, Endymion, pay these respects as readily as though they were copies of his own truth and would knock on the opened Spanish breast. I had circled more words with titles, with nothing. My interference breaks tradition in this respect. Active duty, my logical friend: we then tried a display of retarding method, but were over sagacious. This man quite firmly called out to myself: come abroad.

under the flower
ing hands of the mid
shipman in my charge

under my chest with my love I recce'd
walking in green, mended

by light showers and
the pink flowery skin of several officers,
white by our choice.

I applied to them all
saying, whether we flee ourselves
or force a study of the Spanish
main hope is our full method

second argument

the big ship moves the ordinary manipulations
past. there was in the course of service
mist. the ship went the wrong
way, lacking instrumentation, and I do not choose
to go faster with my tongue.

though I love speed, security
comes from sound observation and attentive
leadership. far behind the scene
she finds once in a Spanish port
where war gives qualified welcome to certain strangers
a Scottish lieutenant

we strolled along the path which overlooks
the town of Coruña
every peasant saluted us

an ally may be loved ceremoniously but is not necessarily a friend
I know you only by the help of my books; fog
placed under cover the original English dispatch

we observed a wine-house crowded with people
thinking this a good opportunity for studying manners
we entered; the landlord
stepped forward with a cup of his best beverage.
of course we drank to the health of Ferdinand the Seventh which
appeared to please them amazingly, for they all shook hands
with us in turn as we took leave.

fourth argument

as much observing war as at war
he was twenty
at 13 entering the navy
his father gave him a notebook
sailor-writer
a Scottish lieutenant in Coruña in 1809
that's the kind of story called history
is that all we need to know about power
looking ahead
what to do with the power crazy
when power is marked out ahead and in another place
as a place of resourcefulness
how does duty play in this
the referred calling – i.e. the call of the sea
may not in the first place
be a call to war
the erotics of ritual power-display
of course clothes are weapons too
in Coruña he goes to the opera
clothed to be desirable
he is my great great grandfather
as such I test him out
somewhere in the forelife of narcissism
'I cannot help remarking how different,
and yet how much alike, the same person may be
at different periods of his life; how much changed
in thought, in sentiment, in action!'

An Alphabet for *else here*, rolled (2008)

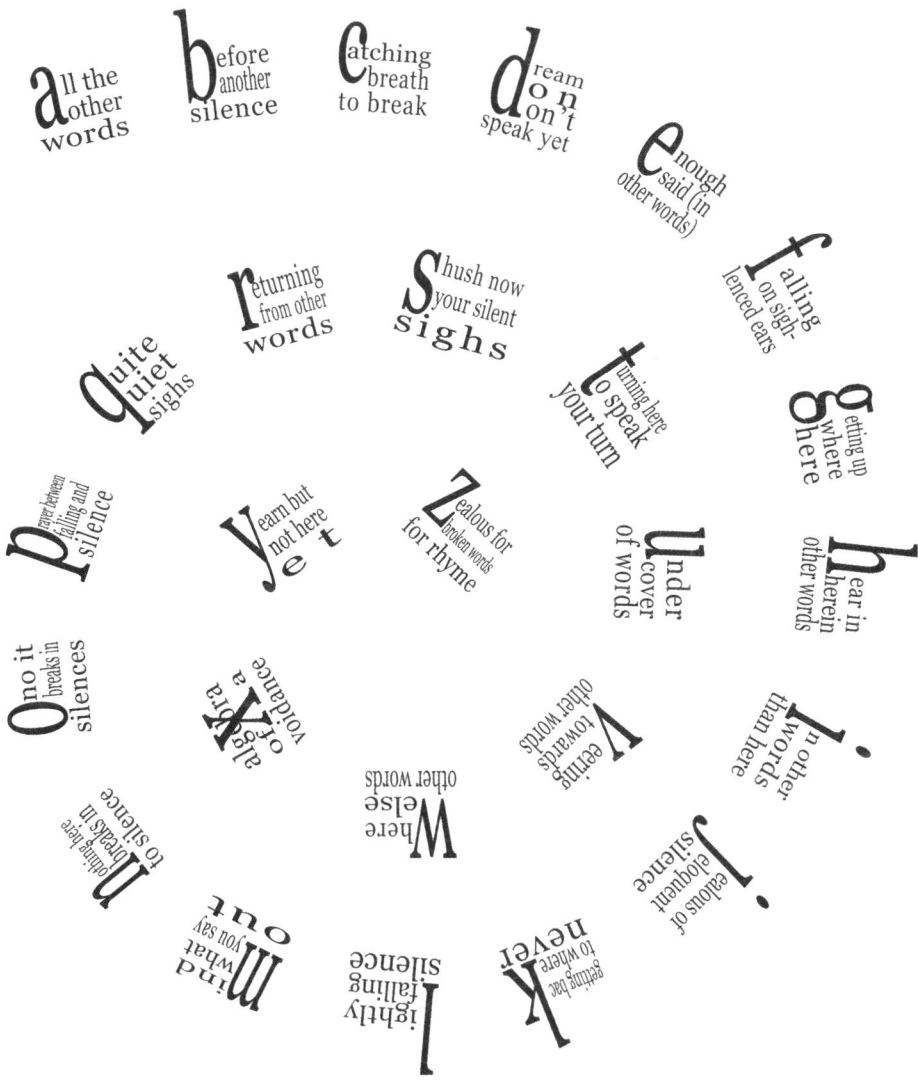

A Coda

Notes on Lyric, polis and love
    For Marianne Morris, her symposium

Come, then, let us create a city from the beginning, in our theory.
Its real creator, as it appears, will be our needs.
                                       (Plato, *Politeia*)

First note (abstract)

    polis
    is ear, throat and tongue
    and the actions that follow
    therefrom

    lyric
    is also lips and palate
    and the actions
    that flow therein

    love
    is arousal
    of attention
    throughout
    for other, others, Other

Second note: lyric

'of or pertaining to song'
    'meant to be sung'
        'expressing the poet's own thoughts and sentiments'
'own' i.e. this poet
    is not knowingly acting as an agent
        for the speech of others not even
first person plural, own-self one step
    away from the city, let's say the polis
        owning-self closing
the gates against the polloi
    (many experienced as mass)
        enclosing the loved ones
wrapped in bonus, hyperbolic monetary reward
    named the good in a transfer of thought and sentiment
        pro bono publico, for action let's say
of mutual good, an act
    that can take the form of song
        as itself act shaping conditions
for other actions, which conditions, for example
    might be the thoughts and sentiments of love
        and the lyric barely recognisable
as itself a full action.
    do the lovers close their door
        on the conditions of the polis
which door the polis, so to speak,
    built. 'There remain then
        only the lyre and the harp
for use in the city, and the shepherds
    may have a pipe in the country.'
busy old fool

Third note: polis

'Greek city-state (especially) considered in its ideal form', that form
        being one we may speak rather than
                inhabit, though perhaps, by speaking, shape. shall we
translate this as 'city-in-speech'
        or the city as it can be
                in the privileged speech of the academy
(i.e. Plato's) or shall we prefer
        'polis-through-speaking', that is
                at any one moment
being brought into being
        through speaking or singing that moment
                of being
passing and folding
        from syllable to syllable in a memory
                that sounds out
in the charged attention of – in that moment –
        a lover, whose listening
                fills both bodies, whose replies do too.
'The body of citizens
        came to be the most important meaning.' not,
                note, the *bodies* of citizens, those singularities.
what one body
        do citizens now have
                where listening and replying, in their folds
enfold, so that social rhythm pulses between one, many, two
        an imaginary unity in
                difference
it is no less a city for this
        singularity
                of the body of the one citizen

    the lover's
             body, the beloved's,
                     the body
of the lyric's
                  singularity.

Fourth note: lyric in the polis

the lyric city of dreadful night
    ungoverned setting for modern life
        is not
the polis-in-speech, that ideal
    and mutually regulated
        community, a dispersed
space of sociality, of multiple others
    whose governance
        is sporadically visible
whose unity is not that
    of those who choose each other
        by talking across a distance mapped out
through telecommunication (letters will do)
    i.e. the work of others
        as a field of cultural congruence
where voices indifferently murmur or declaim
    intimate and public
        one and many
'tell the emperor he is a private man'
    though not perhaps of 'the people'
        that 'body of persons ... viewed as a unity'
though as a term divided
    as between the third and the first person
        and as such subject
like any public
    to multiple privations
        tell the private woman
her privation constitutes
    the res publica
        voiced in the agora.

'The Emperor himselfe,
    who hath no other seat of Empire
        but an Agora or towne of wood,
that moueth with him
    whithersoeuer hee goeth'
        or
'The telegraph and the printing press
    have converted Great Britain
        into a vast agora, or assembly
of the whole community'
    'If any one raise his voice,
        it is audible from Aberdeen to Plymouth.'

Fifth note: love songs

What's the problem?
Do you sing in the polis? Do you sing of the polis? Do your words spoken in the dispersed assembly invoke the qualities of song? Do you sing on your own in the city? Is it easy to sing in time with others, to keep a time that is not your time and not their time but the time that these words – spoken or sung, sung-spoken – bring together? Or is there one who sings on your behalf, to lyre or guitar? Do I mean on *our* behalf? But then which 'our' is, in each case, convened by the song, and could we even begin to call this 'our' a polis? I am there, if I am, because I hear myself there in the words of these others, and I even mouth some of those words, becoming, at that moment, through lyric, the one who also speaks them. Do you find yourself there too? And if so, who exactly are you a you to? This is the question already in its spinning frame, that is *you* first plural, then singular, or the other way round. *Who are you a we with?* I must be plural because I am there and not there, part and apart, sometimes in lyric ecstasy. The melody, that melts me, tears us apart. The I who sings makes the old song her own. It takes a worried man.

What's the problem?
I is the lover, born, it seems, not out of the city's syllables but out of sound and surf. What does the city do about love? Do the lovers, as above, draw the curtains and lock the door on the polis (using the five-lever lock approved by their insurance company). The city has laws about love and the lyric has lores. And 'I' is not only a looking lover (*no such many as mass, only eyes …*), distanced in scopic fascination. Do you see? Do you see now? The lyric lover is lost in sound, where sound shakes the loving body in a shudder of syllables. The city knows this. This is not the place for it. Forget the sounding womb in this place of governance, of law. But then could there be a polis without song, without the old songs?

What's the problem?
A poet of a seaport town sang of the polis. Polis is this, he said. Polis is eyes. No such many as mass, he said, only eyes in each head to be looked out of. *This* – that word, that gesture – is what the one who points says. *This* points, and disappoints, just as *that* does. Now look here. Meanwhile, a wandering European (Canetti) was saying, there are many such manies as masses. Let's be precise about their types. The one who looks and points is at that moment apart, is not of the crowd. So what if polis is not a pointing *this* so much as a circling *this* or an enfolding one; what if polis is *with others*, when who the others are is always plural and always both given and choice. *With others* is a space charged with changing mandates – of demands, of commands, of refusals and systematic negligence as well as of, yes, let's do that together. Do I obey *myself* when I obey your demand? If so, the sting is sweet, for every obeyed command leaves a sting, he said. What else is polis but the social field left by the elders, patterned out of stings of command, of demand? The lover's lyric carries these stings too in its deflected demand, its lightly plucked commands. An order is a counter-love, leaving its sting in the place it counters.

> *These two harmonies I ask you to leave; the strain of necessity and the strain of freedom, the strain of the unfortunate and the strain of the fortunate, the strain of courage, and the strain of temperance; these, I say, leave.* (Plato)

Twenty-six copies of
Keepsache
are lettered A to Z by the author,
and contain an extra poem